Endorsements for the Church Questions Series

"Christians are pressed by very real questions. How does Scripture structure a church, order worship, organize ministry, and define biblical leadership? Those are just examples of the questions that are answered clearly, carefully, and winsomely in this new series from 9Marks. I am so thankful for this ministry and for its incredibly healthy and hopeful influence in so many faithful churches. I eagerly commend this series."

R. Albert Mohler Jr., President, The Southern Baptist Theological Seminary

"Sincere questions deserve thoughtful answers. If you're not sure where to start in answering these questions, let this series serve as a diving board into the pool. These minibooks are winsomely to-the-point and great to read together with one friend or one hundred friends."

Gloria Furman, author, *Missional Motherhood* and *The Pastor's Wife*

"As a pastor, I get asked lots of questions. I'm approached by unbelievers seeking to understand the gospel, new believers unsure about next steps, and maturing believers wanting help answering questions from their Christian family, friends, neighbors, or coworkers. It's in these moments that I wish I had a book to give them that was brief, answered their questions, and pointed them in the right direction for further study. Church Questions is a series that provides just that. Each booklet tackles one question in a biblical, brief, and practical manner. The series may be called Church Questions, but it could be called 'Church Answers.' I intend to pick these up by the dozens and give them away regularly. You should too."

Juan R. Sanchez, Senior Pastor, High Pointe Baptist Church, Austin, Texas

"Where can we Christians find reliable answers to our common questions about life together at church—without having to plow through long, expensive books? The Church Questions booklets meet our need with answers that are biblical, thoughtful, and practical. For pastors, this series will prove a trustworthy resource for guiding church members toward deeper wisdom and stronger unity."

Ray Ortlund, President, Renewal Ministries

Am I Called to Ministry?

Church Questions

Am I Called to Ministry?, Brad Wheeler

Does God Love Everyone?, Matt McCullough

How Can I Find Someone to Disciple Me?, Garret Kell

How Can I Get More Out of My Bible Reading?, Jeremy Kimble

How Can I Love Church Members with Different Politics?, Jonathan Leeman and Andy Naselli

How Can I Serve My Church?, Matthew Emadi

How Can I Support International Missions?, Mark Collins

How Can Our Church Find a Faithful Pastor?, Mark Dever

How Can Women Thrive in the Local Church?, Keri Folmar

Is It Loving to Practice Church Discipline?, Jonathan Leeman

What If I Don't Desire to Pray?, John Onwuchekwa

What If I Don't Feel Like Going to Church?, Gunner Gundersen

What If I'm Discouraged in My Evangelism?, Isaac Adams

What Should I Do Now That I'm a Christian?, Sam Emadi

What Should We Do about Members Who Won't Attend?, Alex Duke

Why Is the Lord's Supper So Important?, Aubrey Sequeira

Why Should I Be Baptized?, Bobby Jamieson

Why Should I Give to My Church?, Jamie Dunlop

Why Should I Join a Church?, Mark Dever

Am I Called to Ministry?

Brad Wheeler

WHEATON, ILLINOIS

Am I Called to Ministry?

Published by Crossway
1300 Crescent Street
Wheaton, Illinois 60187

Cover image & design: Jordan Singer

First printing 2021

Printed in the United States of America

All emphases in Scripture quotations have been added by the author.

Trade paperback ISBN: 978-1-4335-7251-7
ePub ISBN: 978-1-4335-7254-8
PDF ISBN: 978-1-4335-7252-4
Mobipocket ISBN: 978-1-4335-7253-1

Library of Congress Cataloging-in-Publication Data

Names: Wheeler, Brad (Pastor of University Baptist Church), author.
Title: Am I called to ministry? / Brad Wheeler.
Description: Wheaton, Illinois : Crossway, 2021. | Series: Church questions | Includes bibliographical references and index.
Identifiers: LCCN 2021000893 (print) | LCCN 2021000894 (ebook) | ISBN 9781433572517 (trade paperback) | ISBN 9781433572524 (pdf) | ISBN 9781433572531 (mobipocket) | ISBN 9781433572548 (epub)
Subjects: LCSH: Clergy—Appointment, call, and election. | Vocation, Ecclesiastical. | Clergy—Office. | Pastoral theology.
Classification: LCC BV4011.4 .W48 2021 (print) | LCC BV4011.4 (ebook) | DDC 253/.2—dc23
LC record available at https://lccn.loc.gov/2021000893
LC ebook record available at https://lccn.loc.gov/2021000894

Crossway is a publishing ministry of Good News Publishers.

BP 30 29 28 27 26 25 24 23 22 21
15 14 13 12 11 10 9 8 7 6 5 4 3 2 1

The saying is trustworthy: If anyone aspires to the office of overseer, he desires a noble task.

1 Timothy 3:1

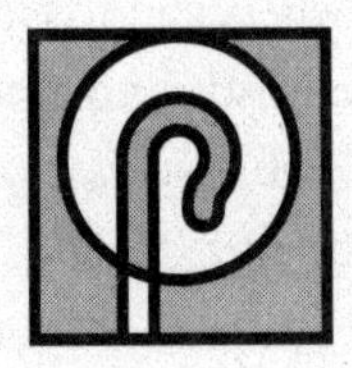

Ministry was the furthest thing from my mind. For some, ascending the steps to a pulpit is the culmination of a lifelong dream. For me, it would have been something closer to purgatory.

I grew up in a loving home, but it wasn't a Christian home. Apart from a few outsized caricatures, I didn't know anything about preachers. And I didn't particularly care for public speaking. Ministry as a "career path"? No way. I had better plans for my life.

As a teenager I was given a Bible and challenged to read it. Prizing myself as reasonably thoughtful and open-minded, I gave it a shot.

Days later, in my bedroom reading through the Gospel of Mark, God saved me.

Scripture slowly began to transform my life, but my view of ministry remained relatively the same. I still viewed pastors as those men who couldn't cut it in the "real world." Clearly anyone with gifts and abilities would get a different job. So you can imagine my surprise when the woman who is now my wife confidently said, "One day, I hope to marry a pastor." Without skipping a beat I retorted, "Well then you'll never marry me because that's one thing I'll never be!" And with a huff, I walked away. *I just showed her.*

Fast forward a few years. I graduated from college and landed a lucrative job in the investment world. For some inexplicable reason that woman married this proud jerk. We joined a small church in the Pacific Palisades of Southern California where the pastor was preaching expositionally through the Gospel of Mark.[1] Week after week, he simply marched through the book, passage by passage.

Yet again, the word of God began transforming my life.

One Sunday, I heard these words slip out of my mouth: "I wonder if that's something *I* should do." My wife looked at me. "You mean manage the church's money?" "No. Preaching," I replied. She was as shocked by my comment as I was.

Even I didn't really know what I meant. So I asked my pastor what I should do if I wanted to do what he did. I'll never forget his answer: "Well, you start by moving to Dallas and enrolling in Dallas Theological Seminary—a fine school, mind you. After about four to six years, you'll graduate. Then look for a job as a youth pastor. If that goes well, you'll graduate to become a young-adults pastor or an associate pastor of some kind. And perhaps after that, you'll become a senior pastor."

I walked away deflated. For a kid growing up in coastal California, Dallas didn't exactly scream "promised land." Neither did giving up a promising investment career for six years of school without a clear path forward seem wise. And starting as a youth pastor? Some might be gifted for this but not me.

Maybe you can relate. Maybe you're a Christian, and for whatever reason, you're thinking about a life in ministry. Should you pursue it? How do you know? What do you do? If so, this booklet is primarily for you.

But it's not only for aspiring pastors. It's also for current pastors and church leaders trying to wade through the murky waters of pastoral assessment. Every week I hear about another crisis in evangelicalism. But there's one crisis that doesn't get any airtime: the scores of men in seminaries convinced they're "called to ministry," who obviously have no business being in church leadership. Seminaries don't raise up pastors, local churches do. So if you're a pastor or church leader, hopefully this booklet will help you better steward your responsibilities before God. Some men you'll need to send out, and others you'll need to keep from going out. Can you tell the difference?

Before moving on, let me make one quick clarification. In this booklet, I'm mainly talking to folks who are wrestling with whether they ought to go into *pastoral* ministry. Much of what I say will be directed at them. But if you're considering giving your life to some other form of ministry, like teaching in a Christian institution or serving in missions, then keep reading! I think you'll still be helped by the biblical principles I'm commending. They easily transfer to your situation.

Let's Talk about "Calling"

One of my favorite films is *A River Runs Through It* (1992). Early in the film, the main character Norman returns home to Missoula, Montana, after six prestigious years at Dartmouth. His proud father, a Scottish Presbyterian minister, then prods him on how he plans to put his education to use.

"I'm not sure yet," Norman tentatively replies.

"You've had six years to become sure," says his father, as a disapproving look sits behind his thin-rimmed glasses. (It seems some father-son conversations never change!)

His father then suggests some advanced degrees in law, medicine, or the ministry, letting that last suggestion of "the ministry" hang hopefully, yet awkwardly, in the air. Clearly terrified at the prospect, Norman blurts out that he's applied for several teaching positions. His father responds in Zen-like fashion:

"Did you find that rewarding? That is to say, do you feel this could be [long pause] . . . *your calling*?"

"My *calling*?" responds Norman, a bit bewildered.[2]

There's a long tradition of Christians speaking of vocations as "callings." This type of language has largely dropped out of use today. Not once during my college years did another Christian ever ask me if I felt "called" to investment consulting. I simply pursued a career in which I could honor God, support a family, and hopefully have some fun.[3]

But there's one vocation where the language of "calling" remains sacrosanct: the ministry. When it comes to ministry Christians still tend to ask, "Am I *called*?" Indeed, you may have picked up this booklet precisely because you read the title and thought, "Exactly! That's what I'm trying to figure out!"

But I'd like to go out on a limb and suggest that "calling" is both an *unbiblical* and *unhelpful* way to ask whether or not you should pursue vocational ministry.

Unbiblical

Asking whether you're "called" to ministry is unbiblical because that's simply not how the Bible speaks of calling. In the New Testament, calling is synonymous with *salvation* not *vocation*.

For instance, when Peter first preaches at Pentecost, he extends the promise of the gospel to "everyone whom the Lord our God *calls* to himself" (Acts 2:39). Peter is clearly speaking about salvation. Similarly, in Romans 8:28–30, Paul affirms that "for those who love God all things work together for good, for those who are *called* according to his purpose. . . . And those whom he predestined he also *called*, and those whom he *called* he also justified, and those whom he justified he also glorified." Calling is a link in that unbroken chain of salvation.

When Paul writes that the "gifts and calling of God are irrevocable" (Rom. 11:29), he's not saying you can never change careers. When he says "consider your calling, brothers" (1 Cor. 1:26), he's not asking the Corinthians to ponder their vocations, but rather who they were at the time of their salvation. Numerous other passages bear this point out. I'd encourage you to look them up and read them for yourself. (See 1 Cor. 1:9, 26; 2 Tim. 1:8–9; 2 Pet. 1:3–4, 10.)

The only clear exceptions to this pattern pertain to Jesus's calling to serve as our high priest (Heb. 5:4) and the disciples whom Jesus called to serve as apostles (Matt. 4:21–22; 10:1), including Paul who was called "to be an apostle" (Rom. 1:1; cf. 1 Cor. 1:1).

In short, the Bible never uses "calling" to refer to what we do as a career; it uses "calling" to refer to who we are as Christians. The apostles are the only exception to this rule. But they uniquely heard a voice no one else could hear (Acts 1:6–8; 22:9), and they uniquely saw visions no one else could see (Mark 9:7; Acts

9:1–9), because they had unique vocations nobody else could share (Eph. 2:20).[4]

As Os Guinness helpfully reminds us, "First and foremost we are called to someone (God), not to something (such as motherhood, politics, or teaching) or to somewhere (such as the inner city or Outer Mongolia)."[5]

But not only is the language of calling unbiblical, it's also *unhelpful.*

Unhelpful

I played a lot of cards in college. Cut me some slack. I wasn't a Baptist yet, and this was before Al Gore invented the Internet. Spades was a favorite game. Spades has "trump cards." You may think you've won a hand. But if another player drops that "trump card," he wins, every time.

This is where our language of calling is not only misleading, but also dangerous.

Just think about the question: "Am I called?" Where's the focus? Squarely on the *individual* asking the question. It has a personal, subjective, even mystical ring to it, perhaps followed by long nights pondering the stars. But nowhere in the Bible is one's fitness for ministry described in such an individualistic way.

And yet, despite the fact that the Bible never speaks this way, I repeatedly find myself in conversations with young men who believe they've been "called" to ministry via some sort of "burning bush" experience with God. Perhaps a young man experiences this "call" at a retreat or conference. His heart is stirred. His mind is racing.

He's now convinced God has called him to ministry. And sadly, while you may observe that he seems to have all the maturity and ability of Shaggy and Scooby-Doo, good luck convincing him otherwise. God's "calling" has now become for him a kind of ministerial "trump card," like dropping the ace of spades. He's been *called*; there's nothing you or anybody else can do about it.

Okay, maybe I've exaggerated *a little*. But the point stands: a "calling" to ministry is utterly foreign in the New Testament. Take Paul, for instance. If there's anyone who could throw down the *calling* trump card, it's Paul. His seminary education began the moment he learned to speak. He had more degrees on his walls than you have books on your shelf (Acts 22:3; Phil. 3:4–6). He actually *had* a vision where Christ commanded him to go into ministry.

But when Paul arrived at the church in Antioch, he didn't flash his apostleship badge and demand everybody else step aside—not in the least. Look at what Luke records in Acts 13:2–3:

> While they [the church] were worshiping the Lord and fasting, the Holy Spirit said, "Set apart for me Barnabas and Saul for the work to which I have called them." Then after fasting and praying they laid their hands on them and sent them off.

Here we see a pattern consistent with the rest of the New Testament (a pattern we'll explore more in a bit). The Holy Spirit set Paul and Barnabas apart for the work, but the local church equipped and endorsed their work. There's a lesson here for us: personal aspiration must be met with a church's public affirmation.

We shouldn't ground our commitment to ministry in some "decisive moment" of subjective calling. We certainly shouldn't encourage others to pursue a "burning bush" experience. If that were required, I, for one, wouldn't be pastoring now. Nor would I be writing this booklet.

In fact, the notion of calling can even be harmful to pastors already in ministry. I heard a local church leader recently say that "because we've been called by God, we can't quit." I think he meant his statement as a "shot in the arm" for tired pastors. But this way of thinking can riddle pastors with unnecessary guilt for leaving the pastorate when it may be the wisest and most loving thing for them to do for their church or their family.

Appealing to a special "calling" can also be used to cloak the inadequacies of unqualified leaders. "Who are you to stand against the will of God?" they'll say, even as a mountain of clear evidence that they shouldn't be in leadership stares them in the face.

So if the language of "calling" is both unbiblical and unhelpful, is there a better way? I believe there is. Instead of "calling," let's talk about the four A's: **a**spiration, **a**ttributes, **a**ptitude, and **a**ffirmation.

Aspiration

I know I've spent the last few pages throwing darts at the overly subjective notion of "calling." But I'm not suggesting that our desires don't matter. They do! In 1 Timothy 3:1 Paul says, "If anyone *aspires* to be an overseer, he desires a noble work" (CSB).

Aspiration isn't just noble (i.e., good), it's necessary!

The Dignity of Ministry

Ministry is a noble task. That's what I missed when I mocked the idea of pastoral ministry as a young Christian. I let the world, and not God's word, shape my views. In my pride, I ridiculed what God deemed reputable and respectable. It's good to desire pastoral ministry because gospel ministry has an inherent dignity. We read in 1 Thessalonians 5:12–13 that we ought to "respect those who labor among you and are over you in the Lord and admonish you, and to esteem them very highly in love because of their work."

The world often laughs at those who would give themselves to preaching "superstitions" and deluding simpletons. My Wall Street boss bemoaned my decision to "throw away a world-class education for the gutters of ministry." His contempt was palpable. Even my own sweet mother wept for weeks when she learned I had made the dreaded jump. Not only was I becoming a pastor, but I would eventually live in *Arkansas*. When all your family originally hails from Boston and is part of the "coastal elite"—I could hardly have aimed *lower* in their eyes.

And yet this laughable and lamentable work is exactly what God deems laudable, honorable, and commendable. I don't regret following his values over the world's (or my family's) values.

The Danger of Ministry

To be clear, aspiration isn't the same as ambition. Many of us inhabit a world of mega-church pastors who live on pedestals. A kind of stardom surrounds the most prominent church leaders. They're the "featured attraction" at the biggest conferences. Like baseball players walking to the plate, some even have their own "walk-on" music as they stroll to the pulpit. They ink the big book contracts. They're surrounded by their adoring fan-base wherever they go. At a large pastor's conference recently, I saw a long line of Christians waiting for one prominent leader to *sign their Bibles*. Did they think he wrote it? I wasn't sure if I should be more shocked at the exceedingly long line of anxious fans with their Bibles or at the pastor *actually* signing their Bibles.

I'm not suggesting that all mega-church pastors are ungodly or self-absorbed. In fact, plenty of small church pastors can be self-absorbed too! I'm simply noting that we live in a celebrity culture—one that has sadly infected the church. We too can become drunk on human personality. How often have I heard captivated congregants refer to their church not by its name, but by its famous pastor. "I go to 'So-and-so's' church." If the last decade of the twentieth century was all about the purpose-driven church, the first decades of the twenty-first century have been all about the personality-driven church.[6] We make messiahs out of our leaders, elevating them to a status of godlike gurus, eagerly hanging onto their every word as if it came from the mouth of Christ himself. At heart, we're all idol worshipers, and we've watched the Lord tear down many of our cherished idols.

My point is that in a celebrity church culture, it can be easy to mistake ambition for aspiration. It's easy to say we're exalting Christ's name, when in fact we won't be happy until ours is exalted too. My father's late pastor used to say, "At every moment, in every relationship, you are either ministering to people or manipulating people."[7] Ministry can become its own form of manipulation where our congregants become the means of our self-exaltation.

Pastoring is dangerous business. We read in James 3:1 that "not many of you should become teachers, my brothers, for you know that we who teach will be judged with greater strictness." Ponder over that a moment. James is warning those who would enter into pastoral ministry. He's asking them to pump the breaks, to bridle that ambition. Because even though pastoral ministry is dignified work, it's also *dangerous* work. So we shouldn't confuse ambition for aspiration. The vast majority of pastors will never have a significant Twitter following. They'll never write a book. They'll never be invited to grace the largest stages. They'll minister in relative obscurity and die in relative anonymity.[8]

Will that be enough? If you're driven by personal ambition, no amount of success will ever be enough. But if you're driven by godly aspiration, you're ever looking to the Savior and saying, "He is enough."

A Gift

Such aspiration is finally a gift of God. It can't be fabricated or manufactured. A brother may be a wonderfully competent pastor and compelling preacher. But if he lacks aspiration, he'll burn out and give up.

As Charles Spurgeon famously remarked, "If any student in this room could be content to be a newspaper editor, or a grocer, or a farmer, or a doctor, or a lawyer, or a senator, or a king, in the name of heaven and earth let him go his way."[9]

Spurgeon was probably employing a bit of hyperbole in order to make a point. I, for one, don't believe the ability to be content doing something else necessarily bars one from ministry. Should we not with Paul learn to be content in whatever circumstances we find ourselves (Phil. 4:11)? The gifting that makes pastors fruitful in ministry would very well make them successful in other professions. Could I be content if I had to return to the investment world? I believe so. It would certainly be easier on my family and my cortisol levels! But at the end of the day, I have one life to spend for Jesus. And for *me*, I felt that needed to be ministry. Perhaps that's what Spurgeon understood when he said "an intense, all-absorbing desire for the work" is a necessary prerequisite to pastoral ministry.[10]

While ministry is spiritually rewarding, if faithfully done, it's also exceedingly *demanding*. The responsibilities are never-ending. Many professions get away with 40–45 hours per week. Pastoring isn't one of them. In terms of cost/benefit analysis, humanly speaking, pastoring is the least rewarding profession one could possibly pursue. Pastoring is *not* a life of ease. When the late-night elder meetings drag on, when emails from frustrated members litter your inbox, when sheep flee the flock or find themselves caught again in the barbed wire of sin, when beloved friends move on and you feel you've bombed another sermon, you'll be tempted to find another profession. Only God-given aspiration will keep one in the fight.

Charles Simeon, a pastor in the eighteenth century, understood this point. Converted in his first term at King's College, Cambridge, he dreamt of one day serving Holy Trinity Church. In 1782, that dream came true.

But most weren't happy with his appointment. Pew holders protested by locking their pew doors, refusing to come, and refusing to let visitors sit in their places. Simeon had to do something, so he rented chairs at his own expense. And then the churchwardens threw them into the street, forcing visitors to stand while Simeon preached. In revolt, the churchwardens also assigned Sunday afternoon lectures to other pastors. No one wanted to hear from Charles Simeon.

This didn't just persist for a month, or even a year, but for over a *decade*. Students threw bricks through windows to disrupt his preaching. Professors assigned exams on Sundays to keep students out of his services. The hostility was considerable and coordinated. Nearly any other person would have folded and given up. But Simeon didn't fold. Spurred on by a mix of stubbornness and godly determination, he persisted in the work—for fifty-four years! He eventually won the congregation over and became one of the most revered and beloved figures in English church life.[11]

Ambition won't fuel such perseverance; godly aspiration will.

But aspiration alone is insufficient. Too many operate as if nothing comes after 1 Timothy 3:1. Paul goes on to describe all that must mark one who wishes to serve in pastoral ministry (1 Tim. 3:2–7). Pastors must not only *aspire* to the ministry; they must also possess godly *attributes*, *aptitude*, and a church's *affirmation*. We must feel *personally compelled* to the work (aspiration), but the church must *publicly confirm* that work in us (attributes, aptitude, affirmation).

Attributes

In his book *Dining with the Devil*, Os Guinness recounts the observation of a Japanese businessman: "Whenever I meet a Buddhist leader, I meet a holy man. Whenever I meet a Christian leader, I meet a manager."[12]

Given our love for efficiency and productivity, and given how we tend to approach life as consumers and treat institutions as providers, it's easy for the church to take its cues from corporate America. So church covenants give way to vision statements. We focus less on what unites us with every other true church throughout history and more on what makes our brand distinct. We measure ministry in quantifiable metrics, and the pastor's job is to grow the "market share." We hire men to serve as pastors who are likable, who can sway a crowd with their winning, winsome personalities.

There are consequences to this: our churches tend to look toward something like the *Harvard Business Review* when it comes to evaluating pastors. We look for charismatic leaders with proven track records. In short, we focus predominately on *giftedness*.

Yet immediately after affirming the necessity of aspiration, Paul highlights a host of godly attributes that must define the gospel minister.

> Therefore an overseer must be above reproach, the husband of one wife, sober-minded, self-controlled, respectable, hospitable, able to teach, not a drunkard, not violent but gentle, not quarrelsome, not a lover of money. He must manage his own

> household well, with all dignity keeping his children submissive, for if someone does not know how to manage his own household, how will he care for God's church? He must not be a recent convert, or he may become puffed up with conceit and fall into the condemnation of the devil. Moreover, he must be well thought of by outsiders, so that he may not fall into disgrace, into a snare of the devil. (1 Timothy 3:2–7)

As many have noted, what's most remarkable about this list is how unremarkable it is. Being self-controlled, respectable, not violent but gentle should mark *every* Christian, not just pastors.

But just as striking is the fact that the Bible prioritizes *godliness*, not giftedness. While many churches tend to focus predominately on *competency*, the Bible focuses on *character*.

The first qualification, "above reproach" (v. 2), is an umbrella term, headlining what follows. The final qualification highlights the same point: "He must be well thought of by outsiders"

(v. 7). Both expressions serve as bookends. Pastors must have sterling reputations both in the church *and* in the community. Church leaders aren't just to be preaching the gospel, but they must also be living pictures of that gospel.

If you aspire to be a pastor, note this carefully. Increasing godliness is more important than inherent giftedness. You ought to be more concerned with your personal maturity than whether you possess the prospects of a prospering ministry.

God cares about your marriage because how you treat your bride says a lot about how you will care for Christ's bride.[13] Pastors must be sober-minded and self-controlled lest they find themselves under the influence of every latest fad and unable to exercise sound judgments in caring for souls. They're "not violent but gentle" (v. 3) because the pugnacious personalities of belligerent bullies bruise Christ's tender sheep.

So ask yourself, Is your life marked by godly character? Are you quarrelsome? Consider your conversations and social media posts. Do you work to promote peace, or are you more prone to pick fights? Tragically, many young men are theological arsonists. They love to start and stoke fires without regard to the extent of the damage they may cause.

Are you hospitable? Hospitality literally means "lover of strangers." Hospitable people seek others out. Do you arrive to church early and stay late in order to engage the stranger and say hello to the visitor? Consider your relationships. Are they all with peers who largely share the same interests and hobbies? A pastor pushes himself outside those walls in order to bring others in.

If you have a family, do they prosper under your leadership? Or do they wither under it? Or, even worse, do they run from it? You can be a capable leader in the community, but if your family life is in utter disarray, your service won't speak well of the gospel. Paul says you learn to shepherd God's family by shepherding your family first.

One area I've seen countless men fail in is sexual purity. Both the world and the church are facing a pornography pandemic. The world may promote it, and your conscience may seek to minimize it, but God says "there must not be even a hint" of it in your midst (Eph. 5:3 NIV). Sexual purity is part of what it means to live upright, self-controlled lives.

Don't be deceived. You cannot be a pastor while also prostrating yourself before the altar of pornography. If you're presently pursuing ministry, you may need to shelve that pursuit so you can get serious about your fight with sin. In fact, such willingness is a mark of one who truly grasps the weight of the office.[14]

Once you're in pastoral ministry, the stakes only become higher. When the consequence is the loss of a job, embarrassment to family, and considerable personal shame, the temptation to hide will be enormous—and the consequences catastrophic. In the famous words of the puritan John Owen, "Be killing sin, or it will be killing you."[15]

All this can weigh heavy on our souls. But to be clear, Paul is advocating personal integrity, not perfection. Maturity, not mastery. Faithfulness, not flawlessness. Leaders in the church must be examples to the church (1 Pet. 5:3). There is no true knowledge of God without godliness (Titus 1:1). If a leader isn't striving after godliness, how can he expect to lead anyone else there?

Love

Beyond the character outlined in 1 Timothy 3, I believe there are two others qualities that ought to mark the heart of a pastor. The first is love because "God is love" (1 John 4:8). Indeed the whole law can be summed up in the command to love (Matt. 22:34–40). Love is the distinguishing mark of the people of God. "A new commandment I give to you, that you love one another: just as I have loved you, you also are to love one another. By this all people will know that you are my disciples, if you have love for one another" (John 13:34–35).

Love marked Paul's ministry. We often think of Paul as a hard-nosed, no-nonsense apostle who tenaciously fought heresy while living a life of austerity. We're grateful for him, but we're not exactly sure we'd want to be besties with him.

But take a closer look. Paul's life was dominated by love. How did he describe his ministry among the Thessalonians? "But we were gentle among you, like a nursing mother taking care of her own children. So, being affectionately desirous of you, we were ready to share with you not only the gospel of God but also our own selves, because you had become very dear to us" (1 Thess. 2:7–8). Paul loved deeply, and that love compelled him to invest himself in the lives of others. So it must be with all who desire to shepherd God's people.

The famous Welsh preacher of the twentieth century Martyn Lloyd-Jones remarked, "To love to preach is one thing, but to love the people to whom you preach is quite another."[16] If you don't love your congregation, you won't sacrifice yourself for them. You'll just use them. Or you'll treat them as a problem to be fixed and not a people to be loved.

Put simply, congregations need to know their pastors love them. And when they do, they'll take almost anything from them.[17] In the words of nineteenth-century pastor and evangelist

Robert Chapman, "My business is to love others, not to seek that others shall love me."[18]

Service

Such love is evidenced in service.

There's been a recent movement to cast pastors in the mold of kings who rule. Pastors certainly exercise authority, and the congregation normally should submit to pastoral authority (Acts 20:28; 1 Thess. 5:12–13; Heb. 13:17; 1 Pet. 5:1–5).

But pastors are called first to an altar not a throne. Pastors must model what it means to follow Christ's words: "If anyone would come after me, let him deny himself and take up his cross and follow me. For whoever would save his life will lose it, but whoever loses his life for my sake and the gospel's will save it" (Mark 8:34–35).

True greatness is found in sacrifice—pastors must model this principle. They shouldn't express worldly machismo or some self-centered swagger and bravado. Jesus says that leaders in his church must not abuse authority like the world's leaders: "But not so with you. Rather, let the greatest among you become as the youngest, and the leader as one who serves. For who is greater, one who reclines at table or one who serves? Is it not the one who reclines at table? But I am among you as one who serves" (Luke 22:26–27).

Jesus takes the world's idea of power and turns it on its head. The revolutionary idea here is that leaders—those who have power, authority, and responsibility—are to exercise it not for their own benefit but for the benefit of others. In God's economy, to lead is to serve. Any who aspire to ministry must aspire to *servant*-leadership. We're to sacrifice ourselves in the service of others.

Pastors aren't kings, but servants of the King.

Aptitude

While Scripture teaches us to prioritize character, that doesn't mean competence is unimportant.

Many professions have exams that test their skills and proficiency. Lawyers have the bar.

Doctors have their boards. Even postal workers are subject to a series of exams. Until you pass, you're not qualified to practice.

Not so in ministry. While some denominations have licensure and ordination requirements, the Bible doesn't create an international credentialing organization whose sole job is to certify a pastor's skillset. But that doesn't mean there aren't specific skillsets, competencies, aptitudes, or abilities necessary for pastoral ministry.

Teaching

One skill that particularly marks out elders from deacons is the ability to teach (cf. 1 Tim. 3:8–13).

Teaching is at the heart of pastoral ministry. A pastor isn't an activities programmer or a personal motivator but a Bible *teacher*. The consistent pattern in Scripture is that God's people gather around the proclamation of God's word (Ex. 24:7; Josh. 8:34–35; 2 Chron. 34:30; Matt. 5:1–3; Mark 1:38; Acts 6:2). Thus anyone who aspires to the office of pastor must be able to teach.

Being "able to teach" doesn't mean you need to be the next Charles Spurgeon. Titus 1:9 further explains what Paul has in mind: "He must hold firm to the trustworthy word as taught, so that he may be able to give instruction in sound doctrine and also to rebuke those who contradict it."

A pastor's opinions must be informed by Scripture, not by culture, tradition, or blind adherence to past practice. Can he open the Bible and accurately explain what it does and doesn't mean? Can he assess a situation and apply the Scriptures so as to effectively guard and grow the sheep? Can he do this in a way that obviously benefits those who listen? If so, then he's able to teach.

But let me offer a quick word of caution. Teaching gifts are developed over time. If you're assessing a man's ability to teach, be careful of making sweeping judgments too quickly. If you're aspiring to ministry, don't bank your future on feedback after one sermon.

My first teaching opportunity came a year after I was saved. I spoke to our youth group. My youth pastor asked me to teach on creation vs. evolution. I agreed only because I couldn't say no to a man who had loved me so well. When it was over, I asked him how it went. After a long, searching pause he said, "It was . . . *thorough*." Translation: reading an encyclopedia entry would have been just as informative and *more* entertaining.

My first sermon came about nine months after I had left the investment world. At the end of the sermon, a woman met me at the door and asked if English was my *second* language. I'm not kidding! That really happened. It was brutal. I wanted to crawl in a hole and die. At minimum, I had to resist the overwhelming urge to call up my old boss and beg for my job back.

I have loads of other humiliating stories. But somehow I survived, developed, and now preach almost every week—some people are even helped by it! But all that took time. My wife said I didn't find "my voice" until after two and a half years serving as a pastoral assistant, seven years of seminary, another five years as an associate pastor, and one year serving as a lead pastor. It was only *then* that I found my preaching legs. At that point, I had probably preached seventy-five or more sermons. So be patient.

Few will be invited to preach a Sunday morning sermon with any regularity. But that doesn't mean you can't begin to develop your teaching gifts. Offer to lead a small-group. Volunteer in the youth group. Gather a friend or two on Saturday mornings and preach to one another, and then critique one another. Invite the pastor or a church staff member to join you and invite their feedback. Consider attending a local preaching workshop. The Charles Simeon Trust program is an excellent place to start.[19]

In his final letter, Paul exhorted Timothy, "Do your best to present yourself to God as one approved, a worker who has no need to be ashamed, rightly handling the word of truth" (2 Tim. 2:15). Though you don't know what tomorrow will bring, there's much you can do today to present yourself as one approved, correctly handling the word of truth.

Discipling

Beyond teaching, pastors must be faithful *disciplers* of others. If *discipleship* is how we follow Jesus (vertically), *discipling* is how we help others follow Jesus (horizontally). Specifically, discipling is doing deliberate spiritual good to someone so they can become more like Christ.

Consider Jesus's ministry. He didn't inaugurate his kingdom with some broad, Madison Avenue mass-market media campaign. Nor did he hire strategists to help him leverage the power of social media or sequester himself in his study reading blogs and ripping-off tweets every ten seconds. He simply gathered a small group of men around him, did life with them, and proactively invested in them over a three-year period.

Discipling defined Paul's ministry with men like Timothy, Titus, and scores of others (Col. 1:28–29). Discipling isn't just hanging out over coffee and catching up. It's deliberately and intentionally investing the word in one another with the goal that we present them mature in Christ. We're not making disciples of ourselves, but disciples of Christ. We labor to make them less like us and more like him. This is how Paul expended his own ministry, toiling and struggling after the spiritual well-being of others.

Pastors aren't preening pulpiteers. They're teachers and disciplers. Paul highlights this point in 2 Timothy 2:2: "What you have heard from me in the presence of many witnesses entrust to faithful men, who will be able to teach others also." Pastoring is about discipling the next generation of pastors and leaders. A man who's not passionately given to this type of work isn't prepared to pastor. Period.

If you're thinking about ministry, ask yourself: In what ways am I currently doing spiritual good to others? Do I invest in others? Am I discipling college students in my church or volunteering to serve at the next youth retreat? Am I strategizing to do gospel work in the workplace? Do I seek out opportunities, or am I waiting for ministry to be handed to me on a silver platter?

In my experience, a prospering preaching ministry in a vibrant church tends to excite young men who want a piece of the action. They may even assume they're "called." But some of them may simply be after a religious job. They assume that if they stand up and handle God's word, *voilà*, people get saved, marriages are restored, children obey their parents, and the lion lays down with the lamb.

But it generally doesn't work that way. Behind every truly thriving ministry lies countless hours of preparation, prayer, and sacrifice. There's simply no substitute for hard work. If you're assessing men, you want to see initiative. You're looking for men who create opportunities and don't merely wait for them.

And when they give themselves to others, what's the fruit? Is it sweet or sour? Do they persevere in relationships, or are they flashes in the pan? Do they have lots of initial excitement and then move on to something else? Such men won't make good ministers.

Affirmation

Okay, so you aspire to ministry, and you think you have the godly attributes and aptitude that's required. But how do you know? How is this confirmed in your life? Is the next step seminary? Ordination?

Churches will have slightly different practices given their ecclesiastical structures. But as noted earlier, I believe that local churches call pastors. At Antioch, Paul didn't commission himself; the church commissioned him. He spent considerable time being raised up in the church (Acts 11:19–30, note especially v. 26), and the church recognized him for the work of pastoring and planting. Though the Holy Spirit called him and set him apart (Acts 13:2), the church sent him on his first missionary journey (13:3). The church, not just the lead pastor or the elders, owned the work.

As a result, Antioch became a "base of operations" for future church planting efforts. The church at Antioch sent Paul on his next two missionary journeys (Acts 15:40; 18:23), and Paul returned to Antioch to report on his work (Acts 14:21). The church that sent him would be the church that rejoiced with him.

Pastoring requires personal aspiration alongside the public affirmation of a local church.

You may be convinced in your mind that you're "called" to ministry. You may feel strongly about your gifts for ministry. But that means very little until a church publicly *confirms* your ministry.

Ordination

Let me offer a quick word on ordination because many identify a particular ordination process as the affirmation of one's pastoral ministry.

The words "to ordain" and "ordination" are not in the Bible. Like many Baptists, I'm somewhat allergic to the word because it conveys the idea that the church has a clerical class. At the very least, we must remember that an ordination certificate doesn't qualify one as an elder for life.

The closest thing to ordination in the Bible is what we find in 2 Timothy 1:6 where Paul mentions that a council of elders laid their hands on Timothy in Ephesus to commission him for gospel ministry. Churches sometimes follow this today when they formally recognize their pastors by publicly laying hands on them and praying for them.

If you're going to use the term ordination, it's critical that you tie it to *the exercise of an office*. Scripture never identifies someone as an elder or deacon who isn't *currently functioning* in that capacity, as with those who leave a church and still refer to themselves as ordained. Disconnecting the two suggests a *status* that supersedes and transcends the exercise of an office in a church. That's one of the central problems with the whole notion of ordination, which, again, is why I don't prefer to use the term.

When it comes to ordination certificates or licensure, states can request them and denominations can use them, but there's nothing in the Bible that requires them.

So What Now?

Perhaps you picked up this booklet hoping for something more definitive. You were looking for boxes to check, some way to easily measure your progress toward the pastorate. Now you're left feeling a bit frustrated. So what now? Let me offer four suggestions.

1. Commit Yourself to a Healthy Local Church

Churches raise up pastors, and churches send out pastors. If you want to pastor, you need to be deeply involved in a healthy local church.

I don't mean to suggest that seminaries are unimportant. They're finishing schools—they should complement what the local church is doing, not supplant it. You don't need a seminary degree to pastor. Some of the greatest pastors and preachers like Charles Spurgeon and Martyn Lloyd-Jones didn't graduate from seminary. Seminaries are, after all, relatively modern inventions. Again, I'm not suggesting seminaries aren't useful. They certainly are! Though the Bible doesn't require them, I do recommend them. Just don't place too much stock in them. And certainly don't mistake them as the *sine qua non* of pastoral preparation.

If you don't have a healthy church in your area, look again. Perhaps you're dismissing some faithful ministries unwittingly. But if not, it would be much wiser to move in order to build your life around a healthy local church than to try to elope into the ministry via seminary.

2. Inform Your Leaders of Your Aspiration

A hallmark of faithful churches is that they're led by men who raise up other men, just like the church in Jerusalem raised up Barnabas and then sent him to encourage and lead young Christians in Antioch. In turn, the church at Antioch raised up Simeon, Lucius, and Manaen (Acts 13:1). Paul did the same thing with Silas, Timothy, Titus, Apollos, Erastus, Trophimus, and scores of others not recorded in Scripture.

Inform your pastors of your interest in ministry so that they can pray for you, mentor you, and provide you with an honest assessment of your progress. But don't assume you'll be fast-tracked. Don't assume every teaching opportunity will now fall your way or that your lunches will be filled with elders pouring into you.

When a man tells me he's interested in ministry, I pray for him, and sometimes that's it.

I can tell he's frustrated. But that's intentional. Sometimes I want to see if he's willing to create ministry, or if he's simply waiting for it to come to him.

3. Get Busy Serving!

Gifts are often discovered in service. So do what's needed to discover and assess how best you're able to serve the church. If you want to teach, start with children's ministry. If you can communicate the Bible in faithful and compelling ways to children, you can communicate it to anyone!

If the church needs a greeter, don't effectively respond with, "I'm sorry you didn't get the memo, but I'm called to *teach*." Don't be that guy! Being willing to serve wherever needed is the hallmark of a faithful minister.

Too many sit around waiting for ministry to be gift wrapped and given to them with fanfare. Start pouring into the life of the church, and trust God will open the right doors at the right time.

4. Be Patient

Jesus spent three years with his disciples. Even after Paul's extensive training in Judaism, he spent another three years preparing for Christian ministry (Gal. 1:17–18). Pastors aren't mass produced on an assembly line.

Preparing for ministry is a process that takes time. Like the best bread, you may have all the right ingredients, but you need time to rise. Trying to speed up the process will only ruin the final product. So be patient. Pray. In the wise words of Edmund Clowney, "It is quite possible to overestimate the gifts you have; it is quite impossible to over-supplicate the gifts you need."[20]

So serve. Wait. And trust that God will complete in you the good work he's begun, wherever it may lead.

Recommended Resource

Bobby Jamieson. *The Path to Being a Pastor*. Wheaton, IL: Crossway, 2021.

Notes

1. Expositional preaching is preaching where the point of the passage is the point of the message and applied to the heart of the hearer.
2. *A River Runs Through It*, directed by Robert Redford (Los Angeles, CA: Columbia Pictures, 1992).
3. Though I confess, not always in that order.
4. See Christopher Green, *The Message of the Church* (Downers Grove, IL: InterVarsity Press, 2013), 217.
5. Os Guinness, *The Call: Finding and Fulfilling the Central Purpose of Your Life* (Nashville, TN: Word, 1998), 31. That's not to say God can't subjectively move in us, prompting us by his Spirit. But it would be wiser and more biblical of us not to employ "calling" language for such promptings.
6. It's worth noting this isn't merely a contemporary problem. The same plague of personality-driven ministry infected the Corinthian church (see 1 Cor. 1:10–17).
7. I'm quoting Tom Shrader here, late pastor of East Valley Bible Church, which is now Redemption Church in Phoenix, AZ.

8. A humbling and yet deeply encouraging testimony of just such a ministry is captured in D. A. Carson's reflections of his father's pastoral work: D. A. Carson, *Memoirs of an Ordinary Pastor: The Life and Reflections of Tom Carson* (Wheaton, IL: Crossway, 2008).
9. C. H. Spurgeon, *Lectures to My Students* (Edinburgh: Banner of Truth, 2008), 24.
10. Spurgeon, *Lectures to My Students*, 24.
11. For more on Simeon see Handley Moule, *Charles Simeon: Pastor of a Generation* (Fern, Ross-Shire, Great Britain: Christian Focus, 2001).
12. Os Guinness, *Dining with the Devil: The Megachurch Movement Flirts with Modernity* (Grand Rapids, MI: Baker, 1993), 49.
13. "Husband of one wife" literally means "one-woman man." I agree with the many commentators who believe Paul is speaking not of *past fidelity* (i.e., Is he divorced?) but *present faithfulness* (i.e., Is he faithful in his marriage?).
14. For more on this topic, see Garret Kell, *Pure in Heart: Sexual Sin and the Promises of God* (Wheaton, IL: Crossway, 2021).
15. John Owen, Of the Mortification of Sin (Fearn, Scotland: Christian Focus, 2012).
16. Martyn Lloyd-Jones, *Preaching and Preachers* (Grand Rapids, MI: Zondervan, 2011), 105.
17. The famous hymn writer and pastor John Newton noted that his congregation would take almost anything from him, however painful, because they knew he meant to do them good. See Sinclair Ferguson, *Some*

Pastors and Teachers: Reflecting a Biblical Vision of What Every Minister is Called to Be (Carlisle, PA: Banner of Truth, 2017), 764.

18. Taken from "The Best Leaders are Often the Least Noticed: Robert Chapman (1803–1902)," *Desiring God*, January 30, 2018, https://www.desiringgod.org/articles/the-best-leaders-are-often-least-noticed.
19. Visit the Charles Simeon Trust website for information on upcoming programs and resources: https://simeontrust.org.
20. Edmund P. Clowney, *Called to the Ministry* (Phillipsburg: P&R, 1964), 30.

Scripture Index

Building Healthy Churches

9Marks exists to equip church leaders with a biblical vision and practical resources for displaying God's glory to the nations through healthy churches.

To that end, we want to see churches characterized by these nine marks of health:

1. Expositional Preaching
2. Gospel Doctrine
3. A Biblical Understanding of Conversion and Evangelism
4. Biblical Church Membership
5. Biblical Church Discipline
6. A Biblical Concern for Discipleship and Growth
7. Biblical Church Leadership
8. A Biblical Understanding of the Practice of Prayer
9. A Biblical Understanding and Practice of Missions
